C000273188

Text: *Stewart Smith*

Series editor: *Tony Bowerman*

Photographs: *Stewart Smith/www. stewartsmithphotography.co.uk, Vivienne Crow, Tony Bowerman, Beatrix Potter Society, Shutterstock, Dreamstime*

Design: *Carl Rogers*

Ordnance Survey Licensed Mapping

Partner

Northern Eye Books

ISBN 978-1-908632-22-7

A CIP catalogue record for this book is available from the British Library.

Cover: *Yewbarrow, Great Gable and Scafell Pikes from Wastwater (Walk 4)*

Important Advice: The routes described in this book are undertaken at the reader's own risk. Walkers should take into account their level of fitness, wear suitable footwear and clothing, and carry food and water. It is also advisable to take the relevant OS map with you in case you get lost and leave the area covered by our maps.

Whilst every care has been taken to ensure the accuracy of the route directions, the publishers cannot accept responsibility for errors or omissions, or for changes in the details given. Nor can the publisher and copyright owners accept responsibility for any consequences arising from the use of this book.

If you find any inaccuracies in either the text or maps, please write or email us at the address below. Thank you.

First published 2015. Revised editions published in 2019 and 2022

Northern Eye Books Limited
Northern Eye Books, Tattenhall, Cheshire CH3 9PX
Email: tony@northerneyebooks.com
For sales enquiries, please call 01928 723 744

www.northerneyebooks.co.uk

 @northerneyebooks

 Twitter: @Stewyphoto
@Northerneyeboo

Printed in the EU by Latitude on woodland-friendly FSC stock

Contents

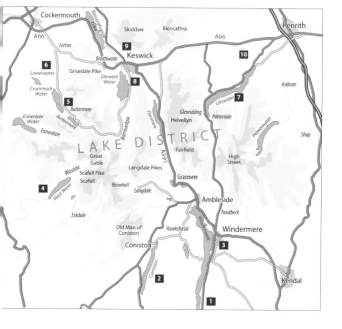

England's Largest National Park

THE LAKE DISTRICT NATIONAL PARK is the largest and most popular of the thirteen National Parks in England and Wales. Created as one of Britain's first National Parks in 1951, its role is to 'conserve and enhance' the natural beauty, wildlife and culture of this iconic English landscape, not just for residents and visitors today but for future generations, too.

Remarkably, the National Park contains every scrap of England's land over 3,000 feet, including its highest mountain, Scafell Pike. Packed within the Park's 885 square miles are numerous peaks and fells, over 400 lakes and tarns, around 50 dales, six National Nature Reserves, and more than 100 Sites of Special Scientific Interest — all publicly accessible on over 1,800 miles of footpaths and other rights of way. It's no surprise then, that the Lake District attracts an estimated 15 million visitors a year.

Looking up Wastwater to the panorama over Yewbarrow, Great Gable and Lingmell

The Lake District's finest views

Most of us would agree that when it comes to hill walking, walks with views are much more fun than those without. They're the walkers reward: the potential grandeur of the panorama from just over the next incline or the atop the next crag is the incentive that draws weary legs to summits. With lakes, rivers, forests, woodland, rolling countryside and craggy fells all crammed into such a compact geographical area, it's no surprise that the Lake District is full of such stunning visual rewards, with unique and beautiful views around every corner.

"I overlooked the bed of Windermere,
Like a vast river, stretching in the sun.
With exultation, at my feet I saw
Lake, islands, promontories, gleaming bays."

William Wordsworth, *The Prelude* Book IV, 1888

TOP 10 **Walks:** Walks to Viewpoints

WHAT MAKES ONE VIEW BETTER than another is rather subjective, but from serene lake shore to atmospheric woodland or wild fell top, there's plenty here to sate most appetites. A grand view usually involves a climb, but that doesn't mean the most strenuous ascents to the highest peaks lead to the best views. The ten walks here have been chosen for the pleasure of the journey as well as the impressive Lake District viewpoints they take you to.

Gummer's How — page 8

Carrion Crag — page 14

Orrest Head — page 20

Wastwater — page 26

The occasionally rocky summit of Gummer's How

Gummer's How

A meander through field, forest and fellside, taking in some of the finest views in the south Lakes

Distance/time: 8 kilometres/ 5 miles. Allow 2½ - 3 hours

Start: Forestry Commission's Gummer's How Car Park near the top of Fell Foot Brow

Grid ref: SD 389 876

Ordnance Survey Map: Explorer OL 7 The English Lakes South-eastern area. *Windermere, Kendal and Silverdale*

After the walk: Mason's Arms, Strawberry Bank, Cartmel Fell, Grange over Sands LA11 6NW | www.masonsarmsstrawberrybank. co.uk | 01539 568 486

Walk outline

This route initially veers away from the intended target to take a circuitous approach on clear paths and farm tracks through forest and open fellside. Passing pretty and peaceful Sow How Tarn, it then takes in the panoramic views from Cartmel Fell, before beginning the steady climb to Gummer's How. The intermediate high point of Birch Fell gives more than a glimpse of the further grandeur of the views to come.

Gummer's How

This route around the higher ground between Windermere and the Winster valley encapsulates the Lake District in miniature. You can expect woodland, quiet lanes, delightful farms and cottages, serene tarns, craggy fellsides and easy paths. Blessed with the advantage of an elevated starting point, it offers excellent views throughout — that only get better as the walk progresses.

Deer may be encountered, but the most obvious beastly sightings will be the Luing cattle that roam Gummer's How as part of an environmental stewardship scheme designed to encourage the regrowth of important vegetation.

Gummer's How sign

Luing cow

The Walk

1. Take the path into the forest at the rear of the car park, signposted 'Sow How Lane'. After 100 metres the path forks at a gate onto the road — take the right hand option veering uphill through the trees, and then out into a felled area. Continue on the path until you reach a gate and turn right onto **Sow How Lane**.

2. Head downhill, through the **Sow How farm buildings**, through a gate and into the field beyond. After 30 metres the track forks — bear left down through the field past the solitary beech tree and through a gate. Ahead and to your left is pretty little **Sow How Tarn**

and its **boathouse**. Stay on the track, crossing the **stone bridge** over the tarn outflow stream, and then through a gate into the adjacent field. Ignore the immediate path to the left, and instead continue straight on for 200 metres through a gate into the forest.

3. Follow the path through this short wooded section, then through a gate into the field. Hug the wall to your right, then curve sharply right then left downhill past what at first glance appears to be another old stone barn, but is in fact **Heights Cottage**, *which until the 1920s was used as a Quaker meeting house.*

Ignore the gap through the wall on your right and head straight on through a gate onto the open fellside of **Raven's**

Pretty Sow How Tarn and its stone boathouse on the eastern shore

Barrow, the uppermost area of **Cartmel Fell**. The faint path curves slightly uphill and round to the left.

A splendid panoramic view over the Winster Valley opens up, with Whitbarrow Scar and the Howgills beyond, and the craggier Kentmere fells further north.

Descend downhill, the path becoming a more distinct track once more, and head through a gate before joining another track at a bridleway signpost.

4. Turn left uphill here, ignoring a fork off to the left as the incline levels out.

Continue on the track through a gate and then an opening through a wall, past a footpath sign and then alongside another wall to your left. Eventually the track turns to tarmac as you pass **Lightwood Cottage**. Go through a gate and turn left on to the road.

5. After 80 metres another lane goes off to the right, and here you'll see a gate ahead with a footpath sign. Go through this into the field and head uphill with the wall to your right until you are close to the top — the highest little outcrop to your left is **Whinny Knott**. Be alert

Panorama over the southern end of Windermere from Gummer's How

for an easy-to-miss **small stone stile** up ahead into the forest. Head over this, before shortly joining a path junction just past a **collapsed stone shed**. Bear right, following this path over a short boardwalk section and uphill to reach a stile over a fence and crumbling wall.

6. Don't cross this; instead, turn left uphill alongside the wall through a (depending on the season) fairly overgrown section. The exact mapped path isn't well trodden here, but being enclosed in a channel between the wall to your right and the forest to your left, you can't stray too far off track. Continue up until you reach the top of the hill and

a stile over a fence, *where all eyes will be drawn north to the view that opens up over the length of Windermere, flanked at its head by the distinctive rugged outline of the Langdale Pikes and the higher fells of the Fairfield Horseshoe to the right.*

7. Continue along the path which becomes more defined, over another fence, and then downhill. *The Coniston fells now adorn your view ahead over Windermere.* Cross a broken wall, a boggy section and join another path. Bear left on this, aiming for the highest point ahead which is the **summit of Gummer's How**, marked by an **OS 'trig' point**.

This dominant position at the foot of Windermere gives commanding views over most of the south and central Lakes.

8. Continue on the same trajectory off the summit on the worn path. It descends rockily downhill, then levels out before you reach a gate onto the road 50 metres uphill from the car park starting point, to complete the walk. ♦

Triangulation points

Like many another Lakeland fell, Gummer's How is topped by a 'trig point': one of 6,500 erected across Britain by the Ordnance Survey to support accurate large-scale land surveying. These hilltop pillars acted as a solid base for measuring instruments called theodolites. Although the trig points' original role has gone, many remain on summits across the country as handy reference points in bad weather — often stumbled across by grateful walkers.

Looking towards Fairfield from the top of Carron Crag

Carron Crag

*A tree-themed-trek through atmospheric forest and open
tracks to an elevated rocky viewpoint*

What to expect:
*Good woodland paths
and forestry tracks,
open fell*

Distance/time: 8 kilometres/ 5 miles. Allow 2½-3 hours

Start: Michell's Coppice Forestry Commission car park, 800 metres
south of Brantwood

Grid ref: SD 309 953

Ordnance Survey Map: Explorer OL7, The English Lakes South-
eastern area, *Windermere, Kendal and Silverdale*

After the walk: Jumping Jenny coffee house and restaurant, Brant-
wood, Coniston LA21 8AD | www.brantwood.org.uk | 015394 41396

Walk outline

*From the eastern shore of Coniston near Brantwood, former
home and now museum dedicated to John Ruskin, this
walk takes you up into woodland and the western fringes
of Grizedale Forest, before taking a circuitous route around
forestry tracks to the upper part of the plantation. It's then a
short direct ascent above the tree line onto the open fell of
Carron Crag, which commands fine views in all directions.*

Carron Crag

The summit of Carron Crag is the highest point between
Windermere and Coniston. Perhaps surprisingly,
Windermere itself isn't visible from the top, but the fells at
its northern end are. The view sweeps anti-clockwise over
a fine array of fells, taking in the Fairfield Horseshoe and
the Langdale fells, amongst others, to reach the Coniston
Fells, which are particularly prominent. The east isn't to
be ignored either, with views over Satterthwaite towards
the distant Howgills. It's a more subtle, but not necessarily
a lesser view, once your eyes have exhausted the more
obviously rugged charms of the views to north and west.

On Carron Crag

Grizedale red kites

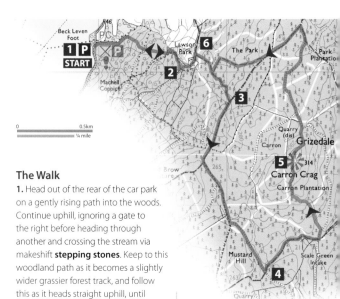

The Walk

1. Head out of the rear of the car park on a gently rising path into the woods. Continue uphill, ignoring a gate to the right before heading through another and crossing the stream via makeshift **stepping stones**. Keep to this woodland path as it becomes a slightly wider grassier forest track, and follow this as it heads straight uphill, until you reach another path at a junction. Turn left on this as it becomes wider and stonier, and weave around, uphill beneath the trees until you reach a hard forest track at another T-junction.

2. Turn left again here, and pass the historic site of **Lawson Park Farm** to your left.

Once owned by John Ruskin, this working farm and smallholding is also the headquarters of Grizedale Arts, the contemporary arts organisation that is probably still best known for the series

of sculptures around Grizedale Forest — some of which can be spotted on this route once you get closer to Carron Crag.

Almost immediately after passing the **farm buildings** and before reaching the garden area, take a right hand path up into the forest once more. As the main path curves around to the left after 150 metres, keep an eye out for a small path off to the right into denser forest. Take

Carron Crag 'trig' point with Wetherlam off to the left

this, and wend your way through this beautifully atmospheric section of thick pine forest until you suddenly emerge onto a hard forest road.

3. Bear right and keep to this main forest track, ignoring a right hand turn off signed for 'Coniston Water' and also a second path beside a signpost, continuing instead as the track curves around to the left; it's signposted for "Satterthwaite". Ignore yet another track off to the right, and keep left again when the track forks before beginning a descent downhill for a short period.

4. Once you begin to head downhill, take the first left turn onto another wide forestry track, now climbing back up again until you shortly reach a crossroads.

Turn left here, ignoring any mountain bike trails that zip off from the main track, then soon turn left on a well worn path uphill into the trees. This is the final climb to the main viewpoint. Wind your way upwards, making use of a few short **boardwalks** to help you over the boggier sections, until you leave the trees and hit open fell for the first time.

Dow Crag, Old Man of Coniston and Swirl How from Carron Crag

The **summit of Carron Crag** features an **OS 'trig' point** atop a rocky outcrop, which should be easy enough to clamber up to for all but the shortest or weariest of legs.

Now finally above the treeline for the first time on the walk, it's worth lingering a while on the summit to take in the entirety of the unobscured views in all directions.

The view is referred to by the Panopticon sculpture near the summit. A panopticon was originally a rounded structure, often in a prison, that allowed inmates to be observed from a central watchtower.

5. Once you're ready to start the return journey, continue on over the summit in the opposite direction to your route of arrival, and follow the path downhill until your feet hit hard forestry track once more, and turn left. Head along this track until you meet another at a T-junction, and bear left again.

After 300 metres, look out for a small path to the right marked by a bridleway sign, and turn right downhill under cover of the trees once more. Follow this path as it meanders downhill, where you now retread over previous footsteps to reach **Lawson Park Farm** again.

6. Turn left past the farm, and retrace

your initial outward route by turning right, down into the woods beyond the farm buildings. Then slant right again off this path to follow your original route straight down the path, across the stream and through the gate back to **Machells Coppice car park** to complete the walk. ♦

'Position, position, position'

This route begins and ends alongside the grounds of Brantwood, former home of John Ruskin and now a museum to the life of the leading Victorian writer, artist, philanthropist and social reformer. Sitting in an elevated and open position above lakeside meadows, the house was built to take advantage of a viewpoint that even early 18th century Lake District visitors considered a must-see highlight.

An ideal seat for contemplation on the summit of Orrest Head

Orrest Head

A gentle transition from town centre to the starting point of Wainwright's famous Lakeland love affair

What to expect:
Short pavement section, urban tracks, woodland paths, grassy fellside

---

Distance/time: 3.5 kilometres/ 2 miles. Allow 1-1½ hours

Start: Windermere town centre opposite railway station. Some street parking on main A591 opposite signposted Orrest Head walk

Grid ref: SD 413 987

Ordnance Survey Map: Explorer OL7, The English Lakes Southeastern area, *Windermere, Kendal and Silverdale*

After the walk: The Elleray, 2-6 Cross St, Windermere LA23 1AE | www.elleraywindermere.co.uk | 015394 88464

Walk outline

Leaving Windermere via quiet paths, with fleeting hints of the views to follow, the route passes through woods, grassy fields and hillside. Views increase in scale all the way, before you round the back of Orrest Head to be presented with the panorama that so enthralled Alfred Wainwright with its promises of the rugged splendour of the Lake District.

Orrest Head

Given the success and popularity of Alfred Wainwright's guidebooks and the subsequent numbers of readers converted to a love of the Lake District fells, a visit to lowly Orrest Head, the place where it all started for Alfred Wainwright, should be obligatory for all Lakeland wanderers.

A diminutive hill it may be, but the expansive view from the summit is worthy of a far more strenuous ascent, and for newcomers looking to get their bearings, a Wainwright illustrated slate plinth helps identify the craggy summits that range across the skyline.

National Trust sign

Brimstone butterfly

The Walk

1. Begin by the main entrance to **Windermere railway station** and cross over the **A591** where beside some railings a large sign proclaims the start of the main route to 'Orrest Head'.

Windermere is the first hopping off point for many visitors to the Lake District, and some are surprised not to be right next to the identically named lake. Originally called Birthwaite, the town grew up around the railway station, which was named Windermere station after the lake.

Referring to the body of water as Lake Windermere to distinguish it from the town is more than a little clumsy, as 'mere' already means a lake. Yet Windermere isn't alone in the name sharing stakes, as Coniston, Buttermere and Bassenthwaite are all 'lakes' as well as villages, too. Bassenthwaite does at least command proper lake status, being the only stretch of water in the Lake District with 'lake' actually in its official name.

Head up this tarmaced track, then after 30 metres turn left on a path signposted for 'A592 Troutbeck Road'. Continue beneath the tree canopy until this path splits. Ignore the right hand option signposted for 'Orrest Head', and instead continue ahead for **Kirkstone Road**.

As you pass a small field to your left, brief shimmers of Windermere present themselves along with Claife Heights and the Coniston Fells beyond. When you emerge on to a private road, go straight across it and take the narrow path beside the large gateposts of **Elleray Bank**.

Ignore any chances to leave this path, most of which are marked as private,

A slate panel identifies the fells visible from the top of Orrest Head

and then shun a path off to the right for 'Causeway Farm'. Almost immediately after this you reach another footpath sign. Bear right here through the iron gate next to the **National Trust sign** and into **St Catherine's Wood**.

2. Continue ahead through this short woodland section, before heading through a gate and out into the field beyond. Head uphill, ignoring a path down to the left, and continue through a gate into the next field. Immediately bear left beside the wall, and follow this round to the corner of the field beside

a gate and footpath sign. Ignore the 'Crosses Farm' option, and instead veer right for 'Orrest Head', keeping to the left of the field as you head uphill.

As height is gained views begin to open up behind you over the head of Windermere, the distinctive Langdale Pikes drawing the eye in the centre of the view.

3. At the top lefthand corner of the field, head through the gate, admire the views to Red Screes and the Kentmere Fells to the left, and then turn right, signposted to 'Orrest Head'. Head uphill on the faint

Coniston Fells, Crinkle Crags and the Langdale Pikes beyond Windermere

track, before crossing a stile, taking note of the two footpath arrow markers and following the trajectory of the leftmost one.

Head steadily uphill following the footpath **marker posts**, and then go through the gate and bear right onto the stepped path uphill which leads on to the **summit of Orrest Head** *with its fine views over the south and central Lakeland fells, as well as the Howgills in the opposite direction.*

The name Orrest is thought to come from the Norse word orrusta, *meaning a battle or clash of armies. It is unclear when*

such a battle may have taken place or the circumstances surrounding it; yet few would dispute it's a view worth fighting for.

4. After savouring the views, continue over the summit, towards the southern end of Windermere, on a grassy path until you come abruptly to a wall. Ignore the seemingly logical right turn, and instead turn left, following the path through **woodland** and over a **stone stile** onto the track.

Turn right here through a gate, keeping to the defined path through the woods. Shortly after passing through a gap through a wall, the path forks.

Take the right hand option signed for 'Windermere A591', and leave the woods through a gate into the field.

Follow the path downhill beside the wall to the far corner of the field, then bear right through another gate onto the track which leads you back to the A591, where a right turn takes you back to the station entrance to complete the walk. ◆

Hill of dreams?

Although Alfred Wainwright named Haystacks as his favourite fell, the view from Orrest Head probably had the greatest influence on him. Arriving at Windermere Station as a young man, and climbing to the nearest viewpoint, he found himself atop Orrest Head. He was enthralled by the 'glorious panorama'. The experience changed his life, leading eventually to the production of his famous Pictorial Guides — which in turn have changed the lives of countless others.

The classic view to Yewbarrow and Great Gable

Wastwater

A low level walk around the lakeshore with tremendous views up the lake to the mountains

What to expect:
Farm fields, open fields, woodland and lakeshore paths

Distance/time: 8 kilometres/ 5 miles. Allow 2½ - 3 hours

Start: Small car park at Cinderdale Bridge, Nether Wasdale

Grid ref: NY 128 038

Ordnance Survey Map: Explorer OL6 The English Lakes South-western area. *Coniston, Ulverston and Barrow in Furness*

After the walk: The Strands Inn, Nether Wasdale CA20 1ET | www.thestrandsinn.com | 01946 726237

Walk outline

A farm track leads away from the road to take you on an idyllic route through fields and then woodland, with hints of the rugged mountain views to follow. Heading beneath Wasdale screes beside the River Irt, you then follow the southern and western shores of Wastwater accompanied by the classic views up the length of the lake towards Yewbarrow, Great Gable, Lingmell and the Scafell massif, before returning via Greendale.

Wastwater

One of England's most famous mountain views, and the one that forms the logo of the National Park authority, is most often reached by car and simply pulling off the road. Such views are, of course, more naturally and satisfyingly appreciated with a gentle reveal by foot.

This route begins by offering you views of the upper reaches of the higher summits as a teaser, before eventually revealing the full length of the mountains top down, with Wastwater itself being the final addition to the classic view

Approaching Wastwater

Raven

The Walk

1. Leave the car park at **Cinderdale bridge** via the entrance and turn right on to the road, crossing over the bridge. Around the corner two footpath signs to the left appear in quick succession. Take the first of these, heading down the farm track with Whin Rigg and the Wasdale screes catching all the attention up ahead. *As you crest a small hill and round the corner, a gate to the left invites you to linger over a taster of the higher mountain views to come.*

Continue on the track through **Easthwaite Farm** buildings and then through the gate where the tops of

Yewbarrow and Great Gable lead you on ahead.

2. After 150 metres on your left you'll pass a gate next to a wall, which is marked private. Ignore this but immediately afterwards leave the track through another gate to the left on the other side of the wall. Continue through this field beside a wall then a hedge, then shortly before reaching the corner of the field bear left through a gate and into the next.

Follow the traces of a path towards **Lund Bridge**, which takes you across the nascent **River Irt**. After crossing this stone bridge, bear immediately right through a gate and into **Low Wood**.

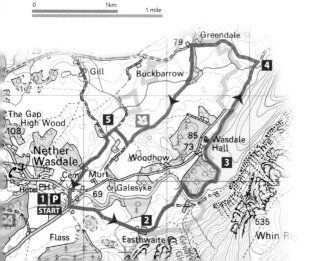

Whin Rigg and the Wastwater Screes on a perfect evening

The path forks instantly, where the right hand choice should be taken to follow the curve of the Irt for a while, until it widens to form an **enclosed pool** beside a picturesque **boathouse** at the southern end of **Wastwater**.

Pass beyond this on the path to soon reach the southern shore of the lake and your first wide open views of the mountains, with the imposing screes and the tricky base path off to the right.

3. Head along the southern shore along the well-maintained stony path, before passing through a gate and past the front lawn of the enviously situated 19th century **Wasdale Hall**, now one of the more grandiose Youth Hostels in the Lake District. Continue through another gate to follow the path beneath trees, and through yet another along the now grassy **lake shore path**, before climbing the wall via a stile and bearing right onto the road.

Carry on until you cross over the bridge and reach a junction, where you need to reluctantly turn your back on the spectacular surroundings of Wastwater to turn left onto the **Gosforth road**.

Yewbarrow and Great Gable from the southern end of Wastwater

4. *There is some consolation as you are now confronted by the fine craggy lower fells of Buckbarrow and Middle Fell up ahead, which would form a more dominant presence over the landscape in most other situations.*

For those with a surfeit of energy, the summit of the latter provides particularly fine views of the surrounding mountains.

For now, however, continue along the road passing through the tiny hamlet of **Greendale**, then head over the **bridge** and turn immediately left through a gate onto a bridleway.

Carry on through the woods beside a field, crossing a **small bridge** as the path curves to the right, then over a stile and into the field. Follow the track ahead through another gate into the next field, then along the path and over the next stile onto a fenced in grassy track.

Ignore a path which leaves to the left and then soon after turn right off the track on a bridleway signed for 'Buckbarrow'. Pass through another gate between two walls before reaching a junction beneath a line of trees.

5. Turn left here, then head though a gate into the field. Aim for another

gate dead ahead, and once through this follow the wall to your left. Keep to this track passing beside **Mill Place** and eventually back onto the road close to your starting point. Turn right then immediately left, signposted for 'Santon Bridge and Drigg', which shortly brings you back to **Cinderdale bridge car park** to complete the walk. ♦

Britain's favourite view?
The vista along the length of England's deepest lake to the mountains surrounding Wasdale Head has been known unofficially as Britain's favourite view since winning a public vote on television several years ago. The view remains a true Lake District icon, and for those unable to climb to the summits of the higher fells, English mountain views don't get much more rugged and imperious than this.

Overlooking Buttermere, Fleetwith Pike and Haystacks from Rannerdale summit

Rannerdale Knotts

A walk that quickly elevates you from Buttermere village to a glorious, grassy ridge amongst craggier higher fells

What to expect:
Grassy riverside path, lake shore, short but steep ascent to a simple ridge walk

Distance/time: 5 kilometres/ 3 miles. Allow 1½ - 2 hours

Start: Pay and display car park in Buttermere village. Some free parking at base of Newlands Pass road above St James' Church

Grid ref: NY 174 169

Ordnance Survey Map: Explorer OL4 The English Lakes North-western area. *Keswick, Cockermouth and Wigton*

After the walk: Bridge Hotel, Buttermere CA13 9UZ | www.bridge-hotel.com | 017687 70252

Walk outline

From Buttermere village this route takes you through fields beside a babbling beck to approach the idyllic shore of Crummock Water, with Mellbreak a dominant presence up ahead. From here, it's time to start climbing, at first on a gently rising grassy path before joining a steeper pitched path to the top of Rannerdale Knotts. Your efforts are then rewarded with a delightful romp down over the ridge ahead, in the company of some fine fells.

Rannerdale Knotts

Rannerdale Knotts is best visited in spring, when its base is surrounded by the purple haze of extensive carpets of bluebells. However, by only paying attention to its lower slopes, many of these seasonal visitors miss out on the best feature of Rannerdale Knotts — its excellent summit ridge, peered down upon by a splendid range of loftier summits.

With Loweswater peeking out from behind Mellbreak to join Buttermere and Crummock Water, the summit also gives you views of three 'lakes', a reward not offered by far more strenuous ascents of many higher fells.

Wainwright memorial

Bluebells

The Walk

1. Leave the car park via a gate at the far end and continue along the lefthand side of **Mill Beck**, avoiding the footbridge across the beck into the campsite. Enter the field via the gate, and stay beside the beck beneath overhanging trees. Ignore a stile and footbridge crossing to the right, and instead follow the fence towards Crummock Water. As you enter a **wooded rocky knoll** you meet another path — bear right on this up and over the knoll and down to the stony shore of **Crummock Water**. *Mellbreak dominates the scene ahead, with Rannerdale Knotts off to your right.*

2. Head right, through the gate, and follow the path, which briefly drifts away from the shore to cross the stream over a **footbridge**. Rejoining the shore, the path then takes you through another gate and over a **footbridge** into woodland. Keep left as the path forks, following it over the wooded headland and through a gate into the field beyond. Follow the

shoreline through this idyllic grassy space, then go through the gate beneath the row of pine trees and on to the road.

3. Head across the road and turn left to join a grassy path which rises gently through bracken. After 250 metres, bear right on a steeper path that climbs towards the crags above. Pause to catch your breath and marvel at the views as the path levels out at a rocky outcrop, before keeping right to ignore the path that descends to the left down to Crummock Water. At a rather sprawling **cairn**, keep right to join a pitched path which ascends steeply between the crags. *The view over Crummock Water to Low Fell and Loweswater provides a handy excuse for rest stops as you climb.*

Crummock Water and Mellbreak seen from Rannerdale Knotts

Continue on the worn path as it bears right around and between more crags, until you suddenly top out onto the **summit of Rannerdale Knotts**.

4. Head along the undulating ridge on a path which is rocky at first, before it turns grassier and begins a steady descent down over **Low Bank** towards Buttermere. As you begin the final descent, bear right on to another path, keeping right as it forks, and continue downhill. As the path levels off slightly, fork left this time to reach another path beside a wall. Turn right on this, then through the gate and out on to the road. Bear left to follow the road back down into **Buttermere village** to complete the walk. ♦

Rannerdale bluebells

Rannerdale Knotts is a rarity amongst hills: one that is overshadowed by its neighbouring valley. The famed Rannerdale bluebells bloom reliably each spring below the fell in a haze of colour. More often found in woodland, this is one of the few areas where bluebells carpet open fell side. A timely summiting of Rannerdale Knotts will give you a unique aerial view of this amazing spectacle.

Crummock Water flanked by Rannerdale Knotts and Mellbreak

Low Fell

A wonderful low fell walk over a rolling grassy ridge, with outstanding mountain and lake views throughout

What to expect:
Easy to follow grassy paths, some small boggy areas after heavy rain

Distance/time: 8 kilometres/ 5 miles. Allow 2½ - 3 hours

Start: Limited parking in small lay-by on the lane just north of Thackthwaite

Grid ref: NY 148 238

Ordnance Survey Map: Explorer OL4 The English Lakes North-western area. *Keswick, Cockermouth and Wigton*

After the walk: Kirkstile Inn, Loweswater CA13 0RU | www.kirkstile.com | 01900 85219

Walk outline

From the small hamlet of Thackthwaite this walk heads up through fields to join a broad grassy path that sweeps delightfully up the flanks of Sourfoot Fell. From here on as you roller coaster over the ridge to Low Fell the views over Crummock Water and surrounding fells are fantastic, the reward far outweighing the effort. Doubling back to explore the opposite end of the ridge at Fellbarrow offers you more open views over the Solway Firth to Criffel.

Low Fell

Low Fell offers some of the best views from a small fell in the Lake District. In fact, it has some of the best views from *any* fell in the Lake District, easily competing with higher viewpoints that demand considerably more effort to reach.

Because you gain most of your altitude at the beginning of the walk, those views also accompany you for most of the way as you move along the delightful grassy ridge. In fact, they're so good, the view from Fellbarrow at the opposite end is almost an anticlimax — though it's well worth a visit, and isn't much of a detour.

'Low Fell' sign

Bilberries

The Walk

1. Head down the lane towards **Thackthwaite**, then turn right, off the tarmac, at **Thackthwaite Farm**, where a footpath sign directs you towards 'Low Fell'. This stony path soon leads through a kissing gate into the field beyond. Head uphill on the right hand side of the field beneath a pleasingly regimented line of overhanging trees, before passing through another gate into the next field. Keep to the left of this one and then at the top of the field head through either the gate or the gap in the wall to join a broad grassy path. Bear right on this, and follow it as it sweeps gracefully to the left around the flank of **Sourfoot Fell**, passing through a gate that would once have allowed you through a now non-existent fence. Soon after, switch back as the path begins to zig-zag more steeply before levelling out and then passing through a gate between the top of **Watching Crag** and the **summit of Sourfoot Fell**.

2. Once through the gate, continue ahead and begin to descend slightly, where your joyous rollercoaster ride along the broad grassy ridge now begins.

The ground falls away to the left giving wonderful views over the Vale of Lorton towards

Descending Fellbarrow with Whiteside and Grasmoor beyond

Crummock Water and its magnificent array of surrounding fells, from Grasmoor and Whiteside to the left, over Rannerdale Knotts and a tiny shard of Buttermere to Fleetwith Pike, Haystacks and Great Gable, the High Stile Ridge then Mellbreak above Loweswater.

The undulating path is easy to follow as it takes you over a stile and then briefly quite steeply uphill. Another bump takes you past a small **shattered cairn** on the right, before dropping down once more to cross a fence via a stile, before a final small ascent to the **summit of Low Fell**,

marked by a **cairn** atop a small rocky outcrop. There are now additional views off to the right over Loweswater, which can be enhanced by continuing ahead and dropping down to a small **cairned promontory** at the far southern end of the fell.

3. Although now as close as you'll get to the Kirkstile Inn which is visible below, to earn your post walk refreshment there's more walking to be done. Turn around to reclaim your outward path and retrace your steps back to the gate on **Sourfoot Fell** at the top of the zig-zags,

Grasmoor, Crummock Water and Mellbreak from the end of Low Fell

then head through it and immediately turn left beside the fence.

4. Almost straight away, bear right slightly away from the fence on the more well worn path to skirt the summit of the fell, dropping downhill to meet a wall and a fence. Follow this to your left, continuing as the wall peters out to climb briefly to the intermediary summit of **Smithy Fell**. Keep to the fence line downhill, crossing over a stile beside a gate to join the left hand side of the fence, which saves you clambering over it further on.

5. Keep to your now familiar fence

companion for the final climb to the **summit of Fellbarrow**, which offers less dramatic but more spacious views than the opposite end of the ridge.

Here the Lake District fells give way to flat pasture and the wind turbine-pricked Solway Firth, with Criffel and the Scottish lowlands beyond.

Hop over the fence and return back downhill alongside it until you reach the first dip, then bear left on a small path towards a small group of twisted and **weather-beaten pines**.

6. Bear left again here to aim for a path downhill through the bracken. As you

reach another **line of trees**, turn left to follow them down hill, crossing over the **small stream** before heading briefly uphill to reach your initial outward route by the gate and non existent fence.

Turn left on the path and then reverse your original route down the path then through fields back to **Thackthwaite** to complete the walk. ♦

'Blue, remembered hills'

The view from Low Fell seems to embrace endless layers of hills: from Mellbreak and the Buttermere fells to Great Gable and beyond. This so-called 'aerial perspective' occurs as the light is scattered by air molecules and minute particles of suspended water and dust. Contrast is reduced, while distant colours become paler and less saturated, and often appear more blue. Experienced together, these effects create a great sense of depth.

Dropping towards St Peter's Church on Martindale Hause

Hallin Fell

A lakeshore and low fell wander, exploring the quieter eastern side of Ullswater

Distance: 5.5 kilometres/ 3½ miles. Allow 2 hours

Start: Bottom of Martindale Hause. Alternative parking available at the top, opposite St Peter's Church

Grid ref: NY 437 194

Ordnance Survey Map: Explorer OL5 The English Lakes North-eastern area. *Penrith, Patterdale and Caldbeck*

After the walk: Sun Inn, Pooley Bridge, Ullswater, Penrith CA10 2NN | www.sunninnpooleybridge.co.uk | 017684 86205

Walk outline

From the base of Martindale Hause a path soon leads you to the shore of Ullswater and views to the open northern end of the lake, before rounding Kailpot Crag to divert eyes to the more enclosed central and southern end. The route then skirts around and up the grassy slopes of Hallin Fell to increasingly reveal the lake's neighbouring layers of surrounding fells, some more famous and well trodden than others.

Hallin Fell

Another small fell with lofty ambitions. When it comes to views, the merits of Hallin Fell are more akin to the stature of its outrageously oversized summit beacon than its actual height as shown on the Ordnance Survey map.

Depending on your favoured kind of view, the eyes can linger over the peaceful twin valleys of Martindale and Boredale, the long, shimmering length of Ullswater, or far over Place Fell to the rugged, higher fells at its southern end.

Summit of Hallin Fell

Wheatear

The Walk

1. From the park at the base of **Martindale Hause**, follow a path away from the road in the direction of Ullswater, signposted for 'Sandwick'. Continue beside the wall until you join another path beside a bench, and keep on in the same direction. Ignore a gate to the right, and climb gently past the house to views over Ullswater and Howtown.

Beneath you you may well see one of Ullswater's steamers making a sedate journey along the lake. Now a permanent part of the scenery, the steamers stop at nearby Howtown (providing an alternative approach to the start of this walk) and have been ferrying visitors up and down the lake for more than 150 years.

As you round the headland, the path leaves the overhead canopy of trees and becomes slightly rockier as you descend to the lake shore, where a couple of stony beaches make excellent snack stops.

2. Head through the gate to find yourself on **Kailpot Crag** — *a fine lookout to the knuckle of Ullswater where it begins to finger its way past Gowbarrow down amongst the high fells of the southern end.*

Cloud-filled Boredale, flanked on either side by Beda Head and Place Fell

Pick up the path again out of the far side of the crag, continuing on an undulating path through eclectic **Hallinhag Wood** amongst beech, oak, mossy rock, fern, bilberry and bramble. Stick to the path until you reach a gate where the end of the wood is in sight.

3. Don't pass through it, but instead veer left uphill beside the wall on a small, steep path through the trees. At the top, head through the gate and out of the wood onto open fellside. The path then snakes through bracken, climbing less steeply around the flanks of **Hallin Fell** beside a wall. *Lake views may have been temporarily left behind, but as the path levels off slightly there are fine views to Beda Head astride Martindale and Boredale.*

Ignore any gates and minor sheep paths to the right until you come to a more major crossroads at the main wide grassy ascent path from **St Peter's Church**.

The church nestles atop Martindale Hause in an idyllic setting. It is one of two places of worship in Martindale. St Peter's is the newer of the two and dates from the

A temperature inversion hides Ullswater from the lip of Hallin Fell

1880s. Further down into the valley is the older St Martin's church, whose present building dates from the 16th-century. Outdating both structures by several long centuries is the ancient yew tree to the rear of St Martin's, which is estimated to be an impressive 1,300 years old.

4. Turn left uphill on this moderately steep path, keeping left as it forks, before rounding a grassy knoll with the unmissable **summit beacon** off to the right. *Here you are reacquainted with views over Ullswater, the additional height treating you to more of the higher fells, including over Place Fell to Helvellyn and its edges.*

The summit cairn, or obelisk as it's referred to on the Ordnance Survey map, originally stood an impressive 12 feet high but over the years its stature diminished as it began to crumble away. It was restored to its full height once more after being rebuilt in early 2014.

5. Pass the beacon and take the left hand path downhill through bracken, bearing right as the path forks, and then right again at a crossroads. Continue downhill in the direction of the church, opting for the lefthand path beside a largely unnecessary **cairn**. Just before reaching the road another path joins from the right.

Follow this briefly, before opting to join the road where the path almost does, beside a footpath sign. Zigzag down towards your starting point — choosing, if you wish, to cut the corners where weary, tarmac-averse legs have done so previously — to complete the walk. ♦

Autumn music

Amongst the shapely hills that form the view over Martindale is The Nab — a conservation area and home to England's oldest native red deer herd. Although you will struggle to see the deer from Hallin Fell, during the rutting season you may well hear them: the bellows of the battling stags echoing down the valley on still autumn mornings. It makes for a distinctive aural backdrop as you wander the fells.

Calf Close Bay, Derwentwater

Walla Crag

A walk to three of the the Lake District's most popular view-points: Ashness Bridge, Surprise View and Walla Crag

What to expect:
Lake shore, woodland, short country lane section, well defined open fell paths

Distance/time: 9 kilometres/ 5½ miles. Allow 2-2½ hours

Start: National Trust Great Wood car park, south of Keswick on the road to Borrowdale

Grid ref: NY 272 214

Ordnance Survey Map: Explorer OL4 The English Lakes North-western area. *Keswick, Cockermouth and Wigton*

After the walk: Dog and Gun, 2 Lake Road, Keswick CA12 5BT | www.dodropinns.co.uk | 017687 73463

Walk outline

This route is essentially one long examination of the splendid view over Derwentwater and surrounding fells from its eastern side. Beginning with a close up from the shore at Calf Close Bay, you then begin a steady climb to the photogenic duo of Ashness Bridge and Surprise View, before doubling back to begin the approach to the high point of the walk — a fine lake and fell panorama from Walla Crag.

Derwentwater

Derwentwater and its surrounding views have been a favoured Lake District destination since Victorian times. Keswick's accessibility by rail and its proximity to a wealth of hills meant easy mountain spectatorship without too much effort or risk. In fact, such is the popularity of this area that you may feel familiar with it even if you've never visited the Lake District before.

The fame of Ashness Bridge has spread to a thousand calendars, postcards, tea towels and chocolate boxes and is an icon of the region that should, quite naturally, be on any viewpoints ticklist.

Ashness Bridge

Bee on heather

Looking down towards the Jaws of Borrowdale and Castle Crag

The Walk

1. Make your way back towards the road from the car park, and head straight across and into the trees, turning left as you meet another path. Follow this for a short while down to **Calf Close Bay** where Catbells sits across the water, resplendent in profile.

As you arrive at the shore at Calf Close Bay, a short detour to the righthand side of the bay brings you to a boulder split into two. This is the National Trust Centenary Stone: a sculpture by the artist Peter Randall-Page

carved from a piece of Borrowdale volcanic rock and placed here in 1995. Engraved on each inner half is an elaborate design of ten segments and ten folded rings, which together represent 100 years of the Trust's work in the Lake District. Due to fluctuating water levels, the stone may be partially submerged or high and dry.

Continue around the wooded headland until you cross a **footbridge** over a stream, and then climb up a rocky section on to the road.

2. Head through the **gap in the wall**

by the layby on the opposite side of the road, bearing left then right around the back of the group of large boulders, and follow the path as it heads uphill towards the base of **Falcon Crag**. When you hit another path, turn right and traverse beneath the crags, *enjoying the constant company of open views over the lake, with Catbells and Maiden Moor prominent.*

3. Eventually you reach a gate; head through this, down to the road and over **Ashness Bridge**, *admiring the famous view back over the bridge to Skiddaw. Being quite possibly the most photographed view in the Lake District means you're unlikely to have it all to yourself, but most people will stop, snap and move on, so you may be lucky enough to catch a space in the traffic.*

From here, continue up the road for 800 metres until you reach twin car parks on your left. Opposite, a gap in the trees at the abrupt edge of the cliff naturally frames the grand vista over Derwentwater that is **Surprise View**. *This is the best viewpoint of the walk so far, the additional height giving a much greater view of the surrounding higher fells than from Calf Close Bay.*

4. Retrace your steps back down the road to Ashness Bridge, on to the same outward path and back through the gate. Here, turn right, taking the higher

level path that leads up the side of the fell through a mixture of bracken, bramble, heather and gorse.

Derwentwater, Maiden Moor and Catbells from Walla Crag

Continue climbing the fell side on this path, eventually crossing a stile over a wall as the path leads slightly away from the lake. Head up on to the rocky outcrop, which is the **summit of Walla Crag**.

This is the highest point of the day, giving an unrivalled full length view of Derwentwater and surrounding fells, with Bassenthwaite beyond.

5. When ready to leave, continue over the summit on a path which skirts close to the edge of the cliff in places, and then through a gate onto grassier fellside.

Head downhill beside the wall, with Blencathra dominating the view ahead. At the bottom of the hill cross the footbridge and turn left onto the lane beside **Rakefoot Farm**.

6. After 200 metres, turn left on to a path signposted for 'Keswick/Great Wood', and cross the **footbridge** over the stream. Head under the trees then alongside the field, *where you are once again reacquainted with views towards Catbells.*

After the field turn left on the footpath signed for 'Great Wood/ Borrowdale' and head into the woods, taking the right

hand option where the path forks. Keep left where the path meets another and continue downhill.

Near the bottom of the hill where the main path begins to curve around to the right, take a small path off to the left which leads you straight back to the car park, to complete the walk. ♦

Through a glass darkly

Although views around Derwentwater may not have altered significantly, early tourists often gained a different perspective using a 'Claude Glass'. Initially a tool of artists, these tinted viewing mirrors simplified scenes and lent them a Picturesque, painterly quality. Users were later mocked for turning their backs on the scene they were viewing — pre-dating the stance of the smartphone 'selfie' generation by more than 200 years.

Helvellyn looming over the flanks of High Rigg

Latrigg

A route that gently elevates you to a fine viewpoint over Derwentwater and its impressive backdrop of fells

What to expect:
Riverside woodland paths, quiet rural lanes, grassy hill top

Distance/time: 10 kilometres/ 6 miles. Allow 2½ - 3 hours

Start: Bell Close car park, Keswick. Lots of alternative town centre car parks if full

Grid ref: NY 266 235

Ordnance Survey Map: Explorer OL 4 The English Lakes Northwestern area. *Keswick, Cockermouth & Wigton*

After the walk: Dog and Gun, 2 Lake Road, Keswick CA12 5BT | www.dodropinns.co.uk | 017687 73463

Walk outline

The route soon leaves Keswick behind, crossing the River Greta to join a delightful woodland path that undulates beside and above its banks. As you begin to approach Blencathra, the path veers away from the river along a quiet lane, before doubling back for the gentle uphill approach to the summit of Latrigg, giving you ample time to begin to soak up the entirety of the grand valley, lake and fell panorama that reveals itself.

Latrigg

Keswick is sheltered among a host of shapely fells and, superficially at least, Latrigg seems to be one of the least alluring. However, once upon it you'll realise why you gave it your attention in the first place. Its tree-lined slopes yield to an open grassy summit, with sufficient elevation to give a wonderful feeling of space as you gaze over a terrific Lakeland panorama.

The woodland approaches are well within the red squirrel stronghold of the northern Lakes, and an early morning wander may well reward you with a sighting or two.

Woodland walk

Red squirrel

The Walk

1. Head out of the car park entrance and turn right on to **Victoria Street**, which continues round the corner as **Penrith Road**. Continue on the left hand side of the road for 600 metres, passing the BP filling station on your right. Shortly after this, turn left at a footpath sign and cross the bridge over the **River Greta**.

Immediately after the bridge, pass through an ungated gap in the wall on the right, and curve uphill to join another wider path. Bear right on this, passing a field to your left, *where the tree lined slopes of your eventual destination of Latrigg loom above.*

Continue until you come to a marker next to a tree directing you left (a private residence is to the right). Head out on to the lane and turn sharply right.

2. Continue along the lane for 200 metres and then turn right into the **riding school** yard, following a footpath sign for 'Brundholme Woods'. At the far right hand corner of the yard a small path leads into the woods. Follow this down the steps until you join another path, finding yourself once again beside the river. Bear left and follow this undulating path for 800 metres until it forks at a footpath sign. Opt for the left hand choice, signed for 'Latrigg', and

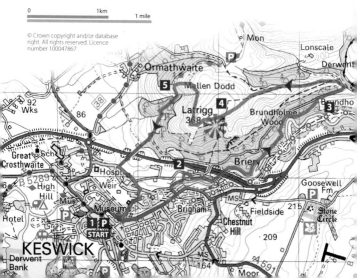

Gazing across Derwentwater to Catbells from Latrigg

follow the path over a couple of small streams via wooden **footbridges**, then head straight across a wider forest track, sticking to the same path. Ignore a stepped path which leads down to the river on your right, and continue until you hit another wider stony track. Turn left on this, following it round uphill to emerge out on to a quiet lane.

3. Turn right, along the lane. Now free from the trees of **Brundholme Wood**, *the fell views begin to open up, and as you climb higher it's worth repeatedly glancing over your shoulder to keep an eye on Catbells and the Derwent Fells as they reveal themselves more and more.*

Once you reach the top of the hill next to a signpost for 'Skiddaw', leave the lane over a stile to the left and head uphill on the broad track. After passing through a fence via the farm gate, bear left off the main track to join a broad grassy path which strikes uphill aiming for the top of Latrigg.

4. Head through another farm gate and stick to the path which skirts the edge of the hill to reach the **summit of Latrigg**.

Keswick and Derwentwater from the summit of Latrigg

Linger here to take in the scale of the expansive panoramic view, from valley to skyline and felltop upon felltop, all immaculately constructed around the shimmering jewel of Derwentwater at its heart.

Once finally ready to take your eyes away from the scene, begin your descent by continuing on the same path, the solitary **bench** at the bend providing another handy excuse to ponder the view a little more.

The path forks at a footpath sign — take the left hand option leading downhill.

After 200 metres, leave the main stony path via a smaller grassy trail down through bracken, and where you meet another track at the bottom next to an information panel, turn left.

5. Keep to this occasionally muddy track as it weaves downhill, ignoring any chances to leave it, and head through the gate at the bottom of the hill next to **Spooney Green** house.

Go ahead over the **bridge** and turn left on to **Briar Rigg**. Follow this road around until you reach the **leisure centre** on your right, and cut a corner by

turning in to the car park and heading round the back of the main building and out on to **Station Road**. Head right, down beside **Fitz Park**, and turn right again at the end of the road on to **Victoria Street** and back to the car park to complete the walk. ♦

Beatrix Potter country

The sparkling centrepiece of the view from Latrigg is Derwentwater, so beloved of Beatrix Potter. As a girl, she enjoyed nine formative summer holidays on the Lingholm estate on the western shore, with its red squirrel-filled woods and rabbit-plagued vegetable garden. Days spent wandering the estate and the surrounding area yielded sketches and notes that would eventually become material for some of her most celebrated tales.

A lonesome pine on the grassy flanks of Great Mell Fell

Great Mell Fell

A short ascent up an isolated fell with wide views to Blencathra and the Dodds

What to expect:
Farm track, grassy paths, fairly steep on the lower slopes

Distance/time: 3.5 kilometres/ 2 miles. Allow 1 - 1½ hours

Start: Small layby at the base of the fell track, just to the north of Brownrigg Farm on the lane between Matterdale End and the A66

Grid ref: NY 407 246

Ordnance Survey Map: Explorer OL5 The English Lakes North-eastern area. *Penrith, Patterdale and Caldbeck*

After the walk: Royal Hotel, Dockray, Penrith CA11 0JY | www.the-royal-dockray.co.uk | 017684 82356

Walk outline

This route initially takes you through woodland around the base of the fell, before striking off on a direct line to the summit through bracken on a small moderately steep path. The bracken can reach neck level in high summer, but the channel of the path remains. The ascent then moderates, levelling off to pass through an small copse of distinctively weathered pine and larch trees, before reaching the small summit cairn atop a grassy mound.

Great Mell Fell

Given the more obvious draw of Great Mell Fell's nearest and more illustrious neighbours — the multi-faceted, rocky jewel of Blencathra to the north west, or the great rolling heights of the Dodds to the south west — there's no surprise it's often overlooked.

Once upon its slopes however, it soon reveals its own unique characteristics, and the gnarled, bowed trees on its exposed slopes make for a wonderfully wild atmosphere as they creak around you on a bleak and blustery day. Its solitary nature and conical shape afford unbroken views around a fine array of neighbouring fells.

National Trust sign

Red grouse

The Walk

1. From the layby, head up the farm track away from the road, then after 100 metres head right over the stile next to the **National Trust Mell Fell sign**. Follow the path beside the fence around the wooded lower slopes of **Great Mell Fell**, where there are views to its smaller sibling Little Mell Fell across fields to your right. The path climbs gently, still skirting the base of the fell beside the fence — buzzards can often be seen circling overhead here.

2. Fifty metres before you reach **Routing Gill Beck** (it should be within earshot after rain), keep an eye out for a small but well-worn path off to the left, and bear directly uphill on this through bracken and thinning trees, where there are views behind you over Little Mell Fell to the distant Pennines.

3. At an altitude of around 420 metres, you eventually wade out of the bracken to find yourself on open grassy fell, *with good views over Matterdale to Gowbarrow off to the left.*

As you reach the **copse**, the path forks. Keep left here and continue through the trees to open fell once more, where another path joins you from the right. Continue ahead to the **small summit cairn** on the shelterless summit, where *Blencathra sits out ahead of you over the now disused rifle range. Views sweep around to the left over the Dodds as far as the fells at the southern end of Ullswater, including Helvellyn, Fairfield and Place Fell. On a fine day the summit makes for a fine picnic spot, but on cold wet days you'll be wanting to grab the views but leave the exposure behind and head off the summit.*

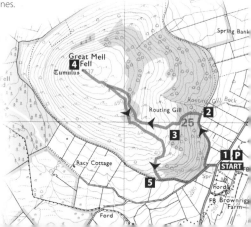

Sunlight streams through the pine copse on top of Great Mell Fell

4. Return initially via the same path, back though the copse, but instead of rejoining the small path that brought you up through the bracken, keep right on the main, broader grassy path. This begins to descend quite steeply, until reaching a fence at a T-junction.

5. Turn left here, following the fence line gently downhill beneath a canopy of oak and sycamore, before crossing over a stile by a gate and onto a wider farm track.

Follow this downhill back past the stile and National Trust sign near the start of the walk to meet the road and complete the walk. ♦

Sacred summit?

The summit viewpoint of Great Mell Fell is crowned by an eroded tumulus, or prehistoric burial mound. The fell's isolation and uniform shape have even drawn theories that the entire hill is an ancient man-made structure. Although this seems unlikely, the tumulus itself probably dates back 4,000 years to the Bronze Age — with the slightly apologetic-looking cairn on top being a far more recent, twentieth-century addition.

Useful Information

Cumbria Tourism

Cumbria Tourism's official website covers everything from accommodation and events to attractions and adventure. **www.golakes.co.uk**

Lake District National Park

The Lake District National Park website also has information on things to see and do, plus maps, webcams and news. **www.lakedistrict.gov.uk**

Tourist Information Centres

The main TICs provide free information on everything from accommodation and travel to what's on and walking advice.

Ambleside	01539 432 582	tic@thehubofambleside.com
Bowness	01539 442 895	bownesstic@lakedistrict.gov.uk
Coniston	01539 441 533	mail@conistontic.org
Keswick	01768 772 645	keswicktic@lakedistrict.gov.uk
Penrith	01768 867 466	pen.tic@eden.gov.uk
Ullswater	01768 482 414	ullswatertic@lakedistrict.gov.uk
Windermere	01539 446 499	info@windermereinfo.co.uk

Emergencies

The Lake District is covered by twelve volunteer mountain rescue teams. In a real emergency:

1. Make a note of your location (with OS grid reference, if possible); the name, age and sex of the casualty; their injuries; how many people are in the group; and your mobile phone number.

2. Call 999 or 112 and ask for the Cumbria police, and then for Mountain Rescue.

3. Give them your prepared details.

4. Do NOT change position until contacted by the mountain rescue team.

Weather

Five day forecast for the Lake District
0844 846 2444 | **www.lakedistrict.gov.uk/visiting/weather-enjoying**